Reinventing the Rules

A Step-by-Step Guide for Being Reasonable

By Lucia Anna Trigiani, ESQ.

Community Associations Press®
Alexandria, VA

ISBN 0-944715-75-3
Reinventing the Rules
© 2002 Community Associations Press™, a division of Community Associations Institute.

Community Associations Press
A Division of Community Associations Institute
225 Reinekers Lane, Ste. 300
Alexandria, VA 22314

To order additional copies of this book, please write to the publisher at the address above or call (703) 548-8600. You can also order online at *www.caionline.org/bookstore.cfm*.

This publication is designed to provide accurate and authoritative information in regard to the subject matter covered. It is sold with the understanding that the publisher is not engaged in rendering legal, accounting, or other professional services. If legal advice or other expert assistance is required, the services of a competent professional should be sought.
　　—From a Declaration of Principles, jointly adopted by a Committee of the
　　　American Bar Association and a Committee of Publishers

Printed in the United States of America

Library of Congress Cataloging-in-Publication Data

Trigiani, Lucia Anna, 1958-
　　Reinventing the rules : a step-by-step guide for being reasonable / by
Lucia Anna Trigiani.
　　　　p. cm.
　　ISBN 0-944715-75-3
1. Homeowners' associations—United States. 2. Homeowners' associations—Law and legislation—United States. 3. Condominium associations—United States. 4. Condominium associations—Law and legislation—United States. 5. Housing, Cooperative—United States. 6. Housing, Cooperative—Law and legislation—United States. I. Title.
　　HD7287.82.U6 T75 2002
　　643'.1'06073—dc21
　　　　　　　　　　　　　　　　　　　　　　　　　　　　　2002009039

Contents

Acknowledgments

AUTHOR
Lucia Anna Trigiani, ESQ.
Troutman Sanders, L.L.P.
McLean, VA

EDITORS
Debra H. Lewin
Community Associations Institute
Alexandria, VA

Christopher Durso
Community Associations Institute
Alexandria, VA

REVIEWERS
F. Scott Jackson, ESQ.
Jackson DeMarco & Peckenpaugh
Irvine, CA

Patricia Harper Martin, CMCA®, PCAM®
Trinity Management Services
Warrenton, VA

David S. Mercer, ESQ.
Troutman Sanders, L.L.P.
McLean, VA

Judy Burd Rosen, PCAM®
The Plaza in Clayton
St. Louis, MO

Kris Cook, CAE
Community Associations Institute
Alexandria, VA

Preface

The best thing—and the worst thing—about community association living is The Rules.

Rules do more to enhance property value and promote community harmony than any other factor. Rules also do more than anything else to enhance negative coverage on the evening news and create division in a community.

In this book, we'll attempt to do away with the worst thing—and promote the best thing—about community living by showing you how to look at your rules from a new perspective. We have intentionally omitted sample rules and boilerplate language from this book because, in order to reinvent rules, community association leaders must start with a blank page. However, Chapter 6 does illustrate our points with detailed discussions of five of the most challenging rules.

In order to help you fill in your blank page:

- We're going to ask you to look at the rules you already have and decide if they're reasonable and *necessary*.
- We're going to ask you to look at the way you apply those rules and again decide if you're being reasonable. Community association leaders sometimes seem to think that making exceptions to the rules or being flexible in their application equates with a failure to carry out their duties to the association. We hope to show you how to achieve a balance.
- We're going to ask you to look at the way you develop new rules and figure out if you're on the right track.
- We're going to ask you look at your procedures and consider ways to make sure they're as reasonable as they are legal.
- We're going to ask you to look at the cost to the community—in dollars and in sense—of battling with residents instead of being flexible and fair.
- We're going to ask you to think in new terms—literally—so that the worst thing about community association living can be forgotten. We've made it a point in this book to avoid words like "enforce," "penalty," "punishment," "power," and other words that have harsh or unnecessarily negative connotations. Yes, it's just semantics, but words have the power to create paradigms—and these particular words have created the policing paradigm, at worst, and the parenting paradigm, at best, that have been so problematic for community associations.
- And, above all, we're going to ask you to be reasonable in everything you do in governing and managing your community association—especially where rules are involved.

That's how you reinvent the rules—by being reasonable.

As you might have noticed, the importance of being reasonable is central to this book. Indeed, the inspiration, jumping-off point, and guiding star for *Reinventing the Rules* is a CAI book with the very title, *Be Reasonable: How Community Associations Can Enforce Rules Without Antagonizing Residents, Going to Court, or Starting World War III*, by Kenneth Budd. Another influence, equally important, is *Drafting Association Rules*, by Gurdon Buck.

Standing on the shoulders of these formative works, the challenge became reinterpreting the basic principles behind The Rules within the context of what it means to be reasonable. It's a challenge that every community association faces today, and one that must be met if we truly want to put our communities first.

**Rules are not
necessarily sacred,
PRINCIPLES ARE.**

—*Franklin D. Roosevelt*

chapter one

Why We Need Rules

Community associations serve a number of important functions in the housing market. First, they offer an affordable place to live. Homes in community associations are typically less expensive, because a developer can reduce costs by clustering units more closely together. Also, community associations offer needed and desired services to residents, such as assistance with individual property maintenance, activity programs, and even concierge services. Community associations also administer and maintain common property—including building components, infrastructure, park-like open space, and recreational facilities. Additionally, community associations regulate conduct and behavior of residents on the common areas as well as in individual living spaces.

These are equally important duties. So, a community association's duty to adopt rules and obtain compliance is as important as its duty and obligation to maintain property. For many reasons, however, having rules and attaining compliance with those rules is both appreciated and dreaded, seemingly in equal measure by association residents.

Why Are Associations Allowed To Make Rules?

Community association rule making has its genesis in the governmental nature of the association. Like a town, city, or county government, a community association has a *charter*—its governing documents. The governing documents are the legal foundation for the community association, establishing the parameters for the various relationships that occur there, including:

- Resident to resident
- Resident to association
- Association to resident

Typically, the governing documents impose on the association the obligation *and duty* to preserve and protect the harmony, architectural

1

integrity, and assets of the community. One of the ways that a community association meets this obligation is by adopting rules and seeing that residents comply with them. In this way, rules are very good things.

Making rules is a serious business and must be approached with care and attention. You can determine what authority you have to make rules by reading your governing documents and asking two questions.

- According to the law and the governing documents, does the board have the power to make a rule?
- What conduct and behavior does the board have the authority to control or restrict?

If the answers to these questions are unclear, be sure to have your association attorney clarify exactly where your authority lies.

Association Rules Are Subject to Law

The rules associations make must be consistent with and comply with existing law—on all levels. When you're considering new rules or reviewing old ones, you need to look at federal, state, and local laws. Rules cannot violate law.

Federal Laws and Regulations

On the federal level, rules may not violate a fundamental right such as freedom of speech, civil rights, and property rights. For example, an association could not enact a no-children rule because it would conflict with the Federal Fair Housing Act. Nor could it specify a no-antenna rule, which would be contrary to federal telecommunications laws.

State Statutes

Most states have enacted legislation that provides a foundation for creating community associations—statutes that apply to condominiums, cooperatives, and property owners associations. States may also have statutes parallel to federal laws—like fair housing—that should be considered.

Local Ordinances

Local ordinances of the town, city, or county where the community association is situated are also a factor. Examples of local laws that you should consider include those addressing pets and pet controls; building restrictions, such as fence and deck height and location; parking and towing; home occupations; and so on. These local ordinances help fill a void in your governing documents, and they can be a useful way to involve local government officials when you're seeking compliance with a rule.

Governing Documents

Likewise, your rules must be based on the authority set forth in your governing documents and must be consistent with them. Rules typically cannot exceed or go beyond governing document authority.

Thus, governing documents empower your board to adopt rules and also to define both the process by which rules may be adopted and the scope of the rules. Perhaps most crucially, they establish parameters for the nature and type of your rules. For example, the governing documents may allow one pet per home, subject to rules adopted by the board.

Rules are expected to amplify and interpret governing document provisions. Absent a source of authority in the enabling statute or your governing documents, a rule will not be enforceable.

Being Reasonable About Rules Is Good Business

How your association makes and applies rules speaks volumes about it as a community. Indeed, your approach to the rules is critical to creating, maintaining, and promoting *community*. It sets the tone for the community and turns a land development into a neighborhood.

The key element, as you've probably realized by now, is *reason*. Reasonable rules fairly and uniformly applied are positive assets to a community. In this sense, being reasonable is just plain good business. Indeed, surveys commissioned by Community Associations Institute show that community association residents are satisfied with their community association home choice—in fact, they would choose to live in a community association again. One of the reasons many of them would make that choice again is the existence of rules.

Why Are Rules Generally Dreaded?

Why is it that rules and the way associations apply them get so much negative press? Besides the fact that we are a society fascinated with law (and that's really what rules are), the stories that have created

National Survey of Community Association Homeowner Satisfaction

Conducted by The Gallup Organization for Community Associations Institute Research Foundation

- **Seventy-five percent of community association homeowners are very or extremely satisfied with their community.**

- **Nearly 40 percent of community association homeowners plan to purchase their next home in a community association, compared to 26 percent who do not.**

- **The number-one reason why homeowners plan to purchase their next home in a community association is upkeep of property (18 percent), followed by safety and security (11 percent). Other common reasons include maintenance of property values, *approval of community rules*, and social activities.**

- **Prime drivers of satisfaction with community association homeownership include overall community appearance, safety, financial accountability, location, and friendly neighbors.**

Though proper exceptions to these general rules are... practicable, yet if the exceptions cannot be agreed on, the establishment of the rules in all cases will do ill in very few.

—*Thomas Jefferson*

> *What causes [people] to rebel is not the assertion of authority but the arbitrary use of power, with little explanation of the rules and no involvement in decision-making.*
>
> —*Laurence Steinberg*

attention are ones where the actions of the association were misunderstood or the association acted unreasonably. If rules are enacted and applied dogmatically, without taking into account the vagaries and variables of human situations, problems arise.

The first thing to remember when embarking on the challenge of adopting rules is that more is at stake than just the rules themselves. That is:

- Developing rules for the sake of having rules is an unnecessary exercise. Develop a rule only if a rule is necessary.
- Rules must be based on proper authority.
- Be reasonable. Rules shouldn't be about limiting the activities of residents or getting back at a neighbor. Instead, they should be about protecting a resident's ability to enjoy the living environment of the community and protecting the value of property from the disruptive or harmful behavior of another resident.
- The focus of rules should be to encourage compliance.

* * * * *

How your association approaches its responsibility to make rules and its obligation to achieve compliance is very important. In this guide, we want to help with the "how"—step-by-step—and, at the same time, encourage you to use rules as a way to maintain and improve community. We hope to answer a few basic questions.

- How do you decide if a rule is necessary?
- How do you know you have the authority to make a rule?
- How do you draft reasonable rules?
- What's the most reasonable and effective way to adopt a rule?
- What are good ways to educate residents about rules?
- What are reasonable ways to encourage compliance with rules?

**That country
is governed best which is
GOVERNED LEAST.**

—*Rutherford B. Hayes*

chapter two

Renovating Old Rules

Believe it or not, our legal system is based on common sense. In fact, at the very beginnings of their careers in law school, future attorneys are often asked to consider what a reasonable person would do under similar circumstances. The "reasonable person" standard is a principle you encounter often when you counsel community associations. Its significance within the context of reviewing, writing, and applying rules is great.

Why is it so important to be reasonable? There may be a number of answers to that question, but the best answer is that reason fosters community. Sure, if a rule is reasonable, community members are more likely to comply with that rule. And, a judge is more likely to enforce a reasonable rule. But, a better argument is that a reasonable rule protects and preserves relationships among homeowners.

Determining whether a rule is reasonable is somewhat intuitive. You know it when you see it. Here are some helpful questions to ask when you review a rule to make sure it's reasonable.

Does the Rule Make Sense?

You want to make sure a rule passes the common sense test. For example, it doesn't make much sense to require cats to be on leashes. Common sense tells us that only one cat owner in a million—and probably no cats themselves—will comply.

Similarly, specifying balcony floor colors for residents of a high-rise condominium makes no sense if no one but the resident can see the balcony floor. But, if the floor is visible from somewhere outside the home, maybe that rule makes sense and is reasonable. Consider your circumstances, then, when enacting a rule.

Is This the Least Restrictive Way To Approach the Issue?

Make sure that the rule is not overly burdensome such that it sets a standard that cannot be met. For example, it's not unusual for condominiums

> *Guilt or innocence becomes irrelevant in ... trials as we flounder in a morass of artificial rules poorly conceived and often impossible [to apply].*
>
> —*Warren E. Berger*

to have restrictions on the color or type of window treatments; in fact, it's a reasonable request. However, requiring every resident to have white vertical blinds with three-inch panels is overly restrictive. The goal is to have a uniform appearance to the building, and that can be achieved by requiring neutral-colored, standard window coverings without micromanaging the situation.

Is the Rule Still Needed? Does It Address a Current Problem?

Is there still a valid need for this rule? You should consider if the rule addresses a current issue or concern.

Take the case of a community whose architectural guidelines say, "No storm doors." The prohibition was implemented at a time when "storm door" meant "aluminum door," and it was understandably intended to prevent residents from installing unattractive metal doors. Today, tasteful, architecturally compatible, and highly energy-efficient, double-pane, sealed vinyl storm doors—or even wooden storm doors—are available. Clearly, rescinding this rule would reduce energy costs and provide residents with more architectural options.

Is It Acceptable to Residents?

It wasn't unusual in the early days of community association development for attorneys and developers to use standardized bylaws documents without much tailoring for individual communities. As a result, bylaws may specify rules for garage doors that don't exist or categorically disallow parking pickup trucks on the street. For community associations in certain parts of the United States, a no-pickup-trucks restriction is very likely to be unacceptable to residents.

Similarly, when one particular community was established in the mid-1970s, the developer filed documents that restricted residents from changing the color palette. Not only is that unacceptable to residents today, but it affects the curb appeal and consequently the value of the community. The association prefers to allow residents to vary the colors. Why not?

Is Compliance Relatively Easy? Is It Possible?

Would a resident who made an effort to comply with this rule find it difficult? For example: "Trash must be placed at the curb before 6 a.m. but not until after midnight." By placing such a narrow timeframe on when trash can be placed at the curb for collection, the association has made compliance difficult, if not impossible. Relax the times a bit to give residents some latitude.

Does the Rule Create New Problems?

You want to make sure that the rule does not produce unforeseen or unanticipated consequences. For example, rules that disallow recreation activities on the common-area lawn might drive residents to play ball in the street or parking lot, creating safety issues or impeding traffic.

Changing With the Times

One of the most visible rule changes was forced on community associations with the enactment of the Telecommunications Act of 1996.

The great majority of community associations have covenants (the best and highest rule) that say, "No antennas, no satellite dishes." When most of those rules were enacted, the 18-inch satellite dish was not yet imagined, much less on the market, nor was digital television or the demand for added TV services.

Circumstances changed. Demand for alternative television providers increased. Recognizing that, Congress enacted the Telecommunications Act and gave the Federal Communications Commission some rule-making authority of its own. Now a substantial number of those no-antenna rules are superceded by federal regulation and are no longer legal or enforceable.

Another indication of changing times is the growing popularity of mini-vans, RVs, SUVs, and "luxury" trucks over the last decade. Developers who filed standard governing documents in the 1970s and '80s disallowing "trucks" could never have anticipated the impact that simple word would have on restrictions in the 21st century.

Is the Rule Getting the Results You Want?

Ask yourself whether the rule is accomplishing your goal—and be sure you've identified the problem accurately so the goal is clear.

For example, one association had a problem with dog piles on the lawn, so it established a rule that dogs could only be walked in a designated part of the common area. After the dog-walking area was created, the association still had a problem with owners not picking up after their dogs—especially in the dog-walking area.

The rule wasn't solving the real problem. The board decided that it was unreasonable to regulate where a dog might relieve itself, but quite reasonable to require pet owners to observe local health regulations requiring them to pick up after their dogs. They rescinded the designated-dog-walking-area requirement and instead endorsed the county ordinance.

Is the Rule Enforceable?

If your association has no real way to attain compliance, you may need to eliminate or restate a rule. For example: "Between the hours of 10 p.m. and 7 a.m. no noise shall be permitted in a unit that measures 30 decibels or greater for more than 10 seconds in the nearest adjacent unit or public area." Who will measure the decibel level and how?

Not enforcing a rule makes the association appear ineffective and arbitrary. Plus, failing to enforce a rule invalidates it anyway, so why even have an unenforceable rule on the books?

> *The truth is that many people set rules to keep from making decisions.*
>
> —Mike Kryzewski

> *The fewer rules a coach has, the fewer rules there are for players to break.*
>
> —*John Madden*

Is the Rule Legal?

Make sure that the rule is consistent with current law. Examples of current laws that are changing and creating compliance challenges are the Fair Housing Act and the Telecommunications Act of 1996.

The best way to go about this is with a legal audit. Ask your association attorney to look over all documents, point out where the discrepancies lie, and recommend appropriate amendments. An annual legal check-up is a good idea if your state legislature is active in adopting rules that affect community associations.

Renovating Old Rules Checklist

Yes	No	
❏	❏	**Does the rule make sense?**
❏	❏	**Is this the least restrictive way to approach the issue?**
❏	❏	**Is the rule still needed?**
❏	❏	**Does it address a current problem?**
❏	❏	**Is it acceptable to residents?**
❏	❏	**Is compliance relatively easy? Is it possible?**
❏	❏	**Does the rule create new problems?**
❏	❏	**Is the rule getting the results you want?**
❏	❏	**Is the rule enforceable?**
❏	❏	**Is the rule legal?**

If the answer to all of these questions is yes, keep your rule. If the answer is no to one or more, maybe it's time to consider an amendment. If the answer is no to a majority of the questions on the checklist, it might be time to consider rescinding the rule altogether.

For all of these reasons, it is important to test your own rules to make sure that they are reasonable. You may want to consider scheduling a periodic review akin to your annual physical; give your rules an annual check-up. What may have been reasonable at the time it was adopted may now be obsolete. Times change, and rules need to change with them.

Cleaning house isn't so hard. Just break it down into three tasks:

• Accept that covenants may become obsolete.
• Adopt rules that are in line with the new law and regulations.
• Rescind rules that no longer comply with new or changed laws.

* * * * *

As with any renovation project, you'll find that some areas will need more attention than others. Some will only need to be dusted off or cleaned up, others will require a new coat of paint. Some will need parts replaced, and some will need to be tossed in the dumpster. Don't be afraid to throw out old rules that are no longer serviceable, or to polish those that no longer sparkle.

'Tis by no means
the least of life's rules:
TO LET THINGS ALONE.

—*Baltasar Gracian*

chapter three

Putting New Rules Into Practice

Rules must be drafted with intelligence and care. After all, your rules are the law of your community. As such, the words that give them life must be chosen carefully. Rules should be clear, concise, and, above all, reasonable. Remember these guideposts when considering new rules:

- Is it reasonable? Compliance will be difficult if it isn't.
- Is it necessary? Making rules for the sake of rules is not the way to go.
- Keep it simple. Avoid legal-sounding words, if at all possible. Make sure the rule is easy to understand.
- Less is more. The rule should be clear and concise. Avoid long sentences and words that aren't relevant.

What Does It Mean to Be *Reasonable?*

A reasonable rule rationally and directly relates to an identified problem or concern and should be drafted to create a cure for or to address the problem or concern. It should be logical and specific enough to cover what's necessary, but not so broad that it offers no real guidance.

The Standards of Reasonable Rules

- Logical
- Relevant
- Rational
- Fair
- Enforceable
- Sensible

Reason has real benefits. If a rule is reasonable, community members are more likely to comply with it. If the rule is an understandable restriction with a purpose, the residents are more likely to appreciate and follow it. If it becomes necessary to get judicial support for a rule, reason is the primary test that the judge will apply. In other words, a judge is more likely to enforce a reasonable rule.

> *There are no rules here— we're trying to accomplish something.*
>
> —*Thomas A. Edison*

Is a Rule *Really* Necessary?

The first question an association should ask when considering new rules is, Do we need a rule? Adopting rules for the sake of having rules is fruitless and frustrating. Rules are generally adopted to address a particular recurring problem or concern.

Before embarking on the challenge of making rules, consider carefully not only the need for the rule and its purpose, but also its potential effect on your community. Let's try to work through the question to find the answer.

Deciding If a Rule Is *Really* Necessary

**Have there been any complaints?
Or, do we anticipate the need for a rule?**

No

Well, then, you may not need a rule.

Yes

Well, we need to consider this a bit more.

How many residents have complained about the problem?

Only 1 resident: Talk to the resident and find out how serious the problem is. Is this an isolated problem? Do we expect this to be an issue with which we will need to deal?

2-5 residents: It looks like this may not be an isolated problem. But, let's take our time and see if this is an ongoing or recurring issue. If it occurs again in three to six months, we may need to look at developing a rule.

5-10 residents: Appoint a committee to investigate and develop a recommendation about the need for a rule.

10 or more residents: Intervene immediately and move forward to enact a rule.

We need a rule — but do we?

- Is there an existing rule that is not being enforced?
- Do the governing documents contain adequate protection without the need for another rule?
- Is this issue regulated by someone else—the city, county, or state?

As the rule-making flowchart shows, whether you make a rule based on resident complaints depends on the number and frequency of those complaints. If you decide that a rule is needed, do a few things first: Research your existing documents to see if the problem is already covered, make sure you're enforcing existing rules, and see if you might be able to get some support from local authorities—if necessary.

Pre-Emptive Rule Making

It's not uncommon for an association to develop rules in anticipation of a future need. In fact, preparing for the future now can eliminate problems later.

For example, a community association may not yet have received any requests to install satellite dishes, but it doesn't take a crystal ball to predict that it soon will. Before the issue presents itself, the board might decide that it should establish guidelines. It's helpful to have a policy in place that instructs residents about preferred satellite-dish placement, color, or safety concerns—before the service technicians arrive. That's reasonable, and it creates community.

Rather than adopt a rule under pressure, why not take the time to think it through before the need arises? We always think better when we have time. Anticipating your association's future needs and establishing rules for them now puts you in a proactive rather than reactive position.

Ripples Across the Community

One of the essential considerations in determining the need for a rule should be its long-term effect on the community as a whole as well as on individual residents. Community associations have been the brunt of much negative press because of over-zealous enforcement of unreasonable or unnecessary rules.

One of the best ways to ascertain what effect a new or refurbished rule might have is to get the community itself involved in the process. Use your existing committees or empower an ad hoc committee to encourage involvement and input from those who will be affected by the rule. A rule that has been developed in an open forum and by consensus will be more effective. People who have a voice in the process will be more inclined to feel ownership of the rule.

Involving everyone means taking advantage of the expertise in your community. The members of your community have a staggering accumulation of real-world experience. Designate a panel of volunteers to research and draft the rule and also to put together the justification for it. Make the process participatory. Listen to your volunteers' advice and recommendations. And, remember to say thank you—privately and publicly.

Get some outside help, too. Turn to your community manager or association legal counsel for guidance. No doubt they have experience in drafting rules. They can offer insight on how they have seen other communities address a particular problem or concern. Take advantage of the several CAI publications on rules, and research for yourself how

> *If you obey all the rules, you miss all the fun.*
>
> —Katharine Hepburn

> *Rules are made for people who aren't willing to make up their own.*
>
> —*Chuck Yeager*

other communities have handled your issue or concern. Take advantage of rules that other people have considered, developed, and tested.

Putting Pen to Paper
The best way to get people reading and keep them reading is to present the content effectively. This means making your rules easy to read and understand, being positive, and letting residents know just what will happen if a rule is broken.

State the Rule in Plain Language
Given a choice, most people will skip the instructions—about almost anything—on the assumption that they're cumbersome and unnecessary.

Rules are instructions on how to live in a community association; if they're cumbersome, residents won't read them. It's important, therefore, to state a rule in plain language, keep it brief, and be specific. Consider the following:

Original:
No signs placed by unit owners or persons other than the association, window displays or advertising, except for a name plate or sign, not exceeding nine-square inches in area, on the main door to each unit and on each mailbox, with the unit number in a form approved by the association, will be maintained or permitted on any part of the common-interest community or any unit.

Restated:
Residents may not place signs on the common areas or in their windows; however, they may place signs that do not exceed nine square inches on their front doors or mail boxes.

State the Rule Positively
Compliance is easier for residents if the rules specify correct behavior rather than just state what isn't permitted. Whenever possible, state rules in positive language; if a rule simply can't be stated positively, encourage voluntary compliance by adding information about what residents can do instead. For instance:

Original:
Section 4.12.b Trash. No garbage cans or trash barrels will be placed outside the units. No accumulation of rubbish, debris, or unsightly materials will be permitted in common elements. Rugs and mops will not be shaken or hung from or on any of the windows, doors, balconies, patios, or terraces.

Restated:
Section 4.12.b Trash. Garbage cans, trash barrels, rubbish, debris, and unsightly materials must be placed in the designated trash-

collection areas at the end of each building, rather than outside units or on the common areas. Rugs and mops must be shaken at ground level at least 25 feet from the building and subsequently stored inside units. In consideration of neighbors, please don't shake or hang rugs and mops from windows, balconies, or patios.

Include the Reason for the Rule

It's human nature for people to ignore or dismiss what they don't understand. If residents think rules are superfluous or gratuitous, they'll ignore them. In some cases it might be helpful to add some clarification. Consider italicized notations that explain why rules exist:

Rule 21.4.a: Residents are required to install and maintain lint filters on their dryers and grease screens on their stove hoods.

Why this rule is important: This rule not only provides for your safety—it also helps keep insurance costs down. In our community the dryer vent stacks and the stove vent pipes are part of the common elements. Built-up lint and grease create a serious fire hazard; by preventing lint and grease from accumulating in the stacks, filters greatly reduce the risk of fire.

Explain the Consequences of Noncompliance

Some people are motivated to abide by rules because they have an appreciation of the consequences. Whenever possible, follow a rule with some information about what a resident can expect in the way of cause and effect.

Original:

In the event a person other than a designated unit owner or his or her invitee parks a car in a reserved space, the affected unit owner (or his or her tenant as designated to the association in writing) may complain to the executive board in writing, describing the date, time, license number, and description of the offending vehicle. The association may have the vehicle towed away as a trespasser, and the association may fine the unit owner of the offending vehicle or his or her invitee.

Restated:

Residents and their guests must park only in those spaces assigned to the unit or set aside for guests by the association. Cars parked in spaces reserved for others may be towed immediately at the owner's expense.

Don't Be Too Specific or Too Broad

The more narrowly focused or specific a rule is, the greater the opportunity for residents to find ways around it, or to inadvertently break it. Similarly, the broader a rule is, the less guidance it provides. Finding a

> *I am free, no matter what rules surround me. If I find them tolerable, I tolerate them; if I find them too obnoxious, I break them.*
>
> —Robert A. Heinlein

> *Rules are for the obedience of fools and the guidance of wise men.*
>
> —*Anonymous*

balance between the two isn't a difficult as it might sound, just bear it in mind as rules are being written.

The Grandfather Clause

When enacting a new rule, you'll need to consider its effect on current residents. Your state may require that you make exceptions for current residents, and courts are more apt to uphold rules that are not applied retroactively. Grandfather clauses are a reasonable way to address the concerns of residents who purchased or selected a home in your association based on certain expectations—that they could have pets, for example, or park their pickup truck there.

However, grandfather clauses present their own set of challenges for an association—primarily maintaining harmony between those who must comply with a rule and those who may ignore it. New residents may be confused and perhaps resentful when they have to comply with a rule that their neighbors blatantly break. "What do you mean, I can't have a dog? The family across the street has one!" A vigorous and ongoing education campaign will be needed so that all residents are aware of the distinction.

Adopting New Rules

The rule-adoption process may be as important as the rule itself. It's so important, in fact, that in some states, if an association doesn't followed certain processes to adopt a rule, the rule is invalid.

What Does Your State Say About Adopting Rules?

Some states have established detailed processes for adopting rules, that, if not followed, invalidate the rule. Check with your association attorney about the legal requirements for adopting rules in your state.

Community associations in many states are given special statutory authority to adopt rules. In Maryland, for example, condominium associations are granted authority to adopt rules—*if* specified procedures are followed. The Maryland Homeowners Association Act does not contain specific provisions concerning rule enforcement; rather, such authority is derived through the general powers and duties granted to non-stock corporations.

After you develop the language of a proposed rule, the process should begin in earnest with public comment from members of the community. The first step is to find an effective way to distribute and publish the *proposed* rule. The association newsletter is an ideal vehicle for promoting and encouraging comment. Public meetings or public-comment periods during board meeting are also good opportunities for input. Web sites are another place to post proposed rules. Just be sure to give adequate time for interested community members to comment.

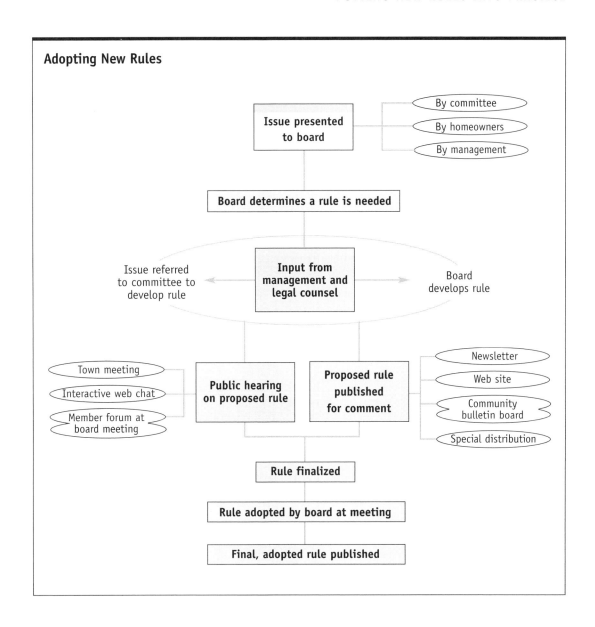

Adopting New Rules

Issue presented to board
- By committee
- By homeowners
- By management

Board determines a rule is needed

Issue referred to committee to develop rule ← **Input from management and legal counsel** → Board develops rule

Town meeting
Interactive web chat
Member forum at board meeting

Public hearing on proposed rule

Proposed rule published for comment

Newsletter
Web site
Community bulletin board
Special distribution

Rule finalized

Rule adopted by board at meeting

Final, adopted rule published

Listen to the Community

Members' comments should be carefully weighed and seriously considered. Your board or rules committee should address each comment and revise the proposed rule to reflect and incorporate relevant input from your residents.

Of course, it's unlikely that the board can incorporate every opinion or position. However, each should be given due consideration. Addressing a comment may entail simply letting a resident know his or her idea was thoughtfully evaluated. Also, don't summarily dismiss an idea as irrelevant or unsuitable because it's contrary to the board's desired course of action. Due consideration means just that.

Adopt It Officially

Once you've fine-tuned it, adopt the new rule officially at a properly convened board meeting. Other meetings—such as an annual meeting—are also good events for adopting new or refurbished rules, particularly those that have generated a lot of debate.

Maintain a clear and precise record of the formal steps you've taken to adopt or enact the rule. This record will be essential later when the association is seeking compliance from residents.

Distribute and Publicize

Once you've adopted the rule, distribute the final, official version to all owners and residents. Publishing the new rules in your newsletter or posting them on your Web site are adequate technically, but distributing copies individually to everyone will get better compliance. That way, you have a better chance that the rule is in the hands of those whose conduct it's intended to regulate.

In conjunction with adopting the rule, the board should give careful consideration to implementing it. In other words, you should consider establishing an effective date for the rule that allows your residents to comply with it.

* * * * *

You'll find that you have the best luck putting new rules into practice if you make sure each one is absolutely necessary, if you keep them as simple as possible, and if you remember—in all things—to be reasonable.

**If the rules
don't work, you
CHANGE THEM.**

—Alan Dershowitz

chapter four

Achieving Compliance

Seeing that all residents comply with the rules is vital to the integrity of an association and has a direct impact on preserving restrictions. Achieving compliance should always be the goal of any procedure an association uses. Forget punishment! Remember compliance.

Common-Sense Approaches to Voluntary Compliance

- *Educate and notify.* Encourage residents to comply by educating them about rules and by giving sufficient notice of the effective date of each rule.

- *Gain consensus.* Take steps to build community consensus to support the rule.

- *Review rules periodically.* Review your rules from time to time, and eliminate or amend them when situations and circumstances change.

- *Act promptly.* Once you're aware that a resident isn't complying with a rule, take action as soon as possible. Failing to act promptly may result in a loss of confidence in the association for some residents or breed an air of permissiveness. Also, the association may lose its right to take action later if violations are allowed to go on too long.

- *Be reasonable with rules and consequences.* The rule itself and the consequences for violation must be reasonable—in the opinion of both the community and the courts. Make sure the consequences fit the situation. Don't use a bazooka when a fly swatter will do.

- *Give residents ample opportunity to comply.* Allow time to fix the conduct or condition.

- *Provide clear information and guidelines on the rule.* The rule must clearly state, in terms understandable to the resident, the behavior that is expected.

- *Be consistent and uniform.* Rules must be applied uniformly and consistently. In other words, the rule must be applied the same way with all residents—taking into account relevant facts that may make circumstances different.

- *Be flexible.* Consistency will be your undoing if you don't allow appropriate and reasonable exceptions.

> *Laws are made for men of ordinary understanding and should, therefore, be construed by the ordinary rules of common sense.*
>
> —*Thomas Jefferson*

Getting the Association Involved

The association should get involved only when a resident has clearly failed to comply with an association rule, local ordinance, or federal regulation. Remember, the association takes action on behalf of the residents who do comply with the rules—not so much as against those who do not. It's not about any one resident—it's about us, the community.

The Board's Role

As a general rule, the board has both the authority and the duty to see that residents comply with all restrictions and rules. However, the way a board fulfills this role is critical to the success of the association. Style is absolutely crucial. One important principle to remember is that going to extremes is never effective. Another important concept—that sometimes gets lost—is that being flexible with rules doesn't mean that you're failing in your duty. Inflexibility can send a simple matter rocketing out of control or result in an expensive power struggle. Work with residents to achieve compliance. Help do good, rather than perpetuate bad.

Committee's and Manager's Roles

The board may delegate all or some of the authority to act on rule compliance to committee, such as the covenants committee or architectural review board. The board can also delegate certain authority to the manager, but do so with care, and check with the association attorney first. Don't leave your manager out there without your support. If you delegate duties to the manager, make sure policy is clear, so that he or she is protected and has the guidance necessary to do the job.

Local Government's Role

Some community association rules and covenants reflect municipal ordinances and standards or, in some cases, conditions agreed to by the developer. In these cases, the association may call upon the municipality to take action, or to be a partner in achieving compliance.

Neighbor-to-Neighbor Disputes

Don't let your board be put in the position of accuser by acting on anonymous complaints. If a resident is unwilling to stand behind a complaint, don't get involved. Or, independently verify the complaint. Remember, just the facts.

Identifying and Verifying Rules Violations

Before following up on a problem with the rules, make sure there really is a problem. There are a number of ways to identify and verify rule violations.

Gather the Facts

The board must be careful to consider all relevant factors and to deal with factual information. Verify facts with a personal visit or an independent inquiry.

Conduct Periodic Physical Inspections

The board, manager, or appropriate committees should periodically inspect the property. This should include routine inspections of approved architectural applications, as well as other compliance concerns.

Resident Input

Residents will alert an association to rules violations—most often in the form of a complaint—but not always. Ask and encourage, and even require, these to be submitted in writing. Then check to make sure the complaint contains an accurate description and specific details of the time and place of the alleged violation. Pictures are a bonus.

Verify Complaints

To the extent possible, the managing agent or an association representative should confirm the violation. Their observations should be submitted in writing and attached to the complaint. Photographs, noting dates and times, if appropriate, should be included. Again, make your own inspection.

Achieving Compliance Informally

The informal approach is a positive and effective way to gain voluntary compliance, and should be your first step. It can help avoid expensive litigation and secure compliance in a neighborly fashion—because compliance is what it's all about.

Personal Contact

Achieving compliance may be as simple as a conversation between neighbors or some kind of communication between the association and the resident. Remember that the tone of the communication is a trigger for the response.

Start with a simple personal call or a visit. Particularly in small communities, a phone call or a knock on the door with a friendly reminder and an appeal for compliance may be all that's needed. You may find that the resident is genuinely unaware of a particular rule or that there are extenuating circumstances to be considered—perhaps something the association can help with. How many times have we heard, "I had no idea. If you'd called me, I wouldn't have done that."

This promotes a sense of community and fosters cooperation among residents, who will see their managers and board members as caring neighbors and leaders rather than enforcers.

The First Written Notice

If a casual conversation doesn't work, or if you're unable to reach the resident, you may need to send something through the mail. Start with a friendly, polite letter explaining the violation. It's important that this letter be positive and allow the resident the benefit of the doubt. E-mail works, too. But the tone of the e-mail communication must be carefully checked and re-checked.

> *If moral behavior were simply following rules, we could program a computer to be moral.*
>
> —*Samuel P. Ginder*

> *The mind demands rules; the facts demand exceptions.*
>
> —*Mason Cooley*

Making Exceptions

Occasionally, after discussing a violation with a resident, you might discover an unusual situation or unique problem that begs for an exception to the rule. Because exceptions *may* weaken a rule, boards are naturally reluctant to make them. But failing to make an exception—under exceptional circumstances—is not the way to be reasonable. Furthermore, sometimes not making the exception results in greater harm to the entire community. If exceptions become the rule, maybe it's time to amend or repeal the rule.

Exceptions should not be granted because enforcement is impractical, inconvenient, bothersome, or expensive. If these conditions exist, reexamine the rule and make appropriate changes. Exceptions should be extremely rare, but not unheard of. For all other violations, consistency is essential to success.

Consistency

Whether raising children, training dogs, or managing community associations, everyone agrees that consistency is of the utmost importance. Associations have an obligation to treat all residents alike, especially when applying rules. In addition to meeting this legal obligation, the board should also meet its obligation to promote harmony and community spirit. Inconsistent application of the rules invariably divides residents and promotes discord.

If a problem ends up in court, nothing will lose the association's case faster than evidence that the rule hasn't been applied consistently. This happened to a Mississippi association that sued a resident for building—and refusing to remove—a fence in its no-fences community.

Facilitating Compliance Informally

❑ Obtain resident complaints in writing.

❑ Gather all the facts and verify the complaint.

❑ Document problems in writing and with photos, if appropriate.

❑ Check the resolutions and governing documents.

❑ Contact the resident in question personally; discuss the problem casually.

❑ Determine the most reasonable way to approach the problem.

❑ Consider the resident's circumstances, and determine if the association can help.

❑ Consider whether making an exception would be in the association's best interests.

❑ Follow personal contact with written documentation.

❑ Send a friendly follow-up letter to the resident.

❑ Contact the municipality or local government—if applicable.

❑ Send a second, stronger letter if necessary.

Unfortunately, there were a lot of fences throughout the community, leaving the association in an indefensible position. Rather than achieving compliance, the association agitated the community and spent a lot of money on legal fees.

The Grace Period

If you're enacting a new rule, amending an old one, or just beefing up your compliance efforts, give residents time to adjust. For some, compliance might require some creative problem solving, and that can take a little time. Set your implementation date far enough in the future that the association has adequate time to notify all residents—repeatedly—of the change, and that they have adequate time to make it. After the rule goes into effect, set aside a time (30, 60, 90 days) where only warnings are issued.

Formal Enforcement

Sometimes friendly, informal methods to gain compliance with rules just don't get results. When the informal approach comes up short, you'll have to use more formal means. Getting formal means following due process, to protect the rights of residents as well as the association.

The Seven Deadly Sins of Enforcement

1. Regulating the personal lives of residents.

2. Giving in to political pressure.

3. Going to extremes.

4. Imposing harsh consequences for small infractions.

5. Failing to make exceptions in exceptional circumstances.

6. Acting on anonymous, unverified, or unsubstantiated complaints.

7. Failing to be flexible, creative, and reasonable.

Due Process

Due process is a legal term that means simply basic fairness. The person who is alleged to have violated a rule must be treated fairly and afforded basic due-process rights.

Develop Due-Process Procedures

The best way to assure that a resident's due-process rights are uniformly respected is to develop a standard rule-enforcement or due-process procedure and apply it consistently. This procedure is itself a rule. So, like other rules, it should be reasonable and adopted after public comment.

The governing documents and the statutes that govern your community association should offer guidelines for developing due-process procedures.

> *The executive exists to make sensible exceptions to general rules.*
>
> —*Elting E. Morison*

27

Due-Process Procedure

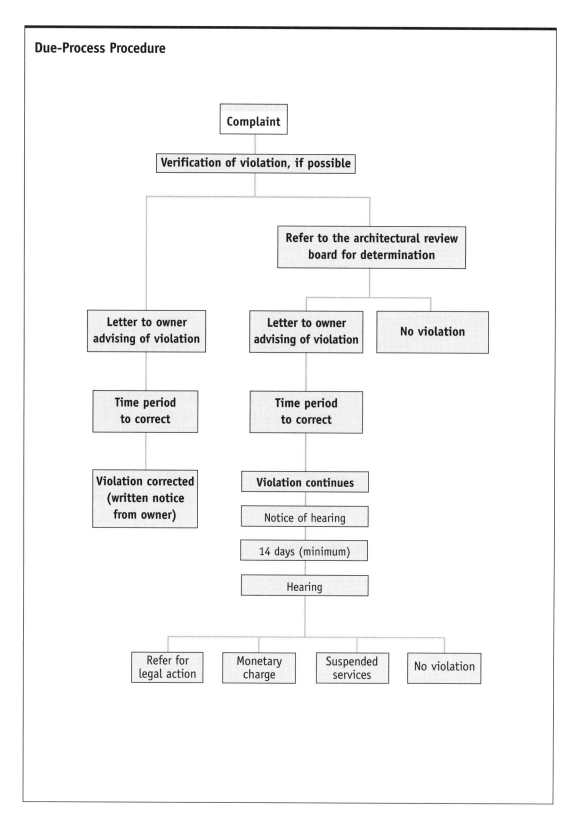

The Essentials of Due Process

The essential elements of due process must be part of the rule-enforcement procedure: *Notice*, opportunity for *hearing*, and the opportunity to be *represented* by legal counsel.

> **Essentials of Due Process**
> - **Give notice.**
> - **Provide an opportunity to be heard.**
> - **All parties have the right to be represented by legal counsel.**

Notice. Providing notice to a resident of a rule violation is the first step—and an essential ingredient—in due process. It should be in writing, and it must contain certain information:
- A description of the alleged rule violation.
- A restatement of the rule.
- The possible penalty.
- A request for specific action by the resident by a specific date as a way of encouraging voluntary compliance.
- Action that may be taken if the violation is not corrected within the time established in the notice.
- The opportunity to appear before the appropriate authority to offer a defense against the charge.
- The consequences of not appearing before the appropriate authority.

Hearing. The board or a designated association committee (often, it's the covenants committee or architectural review board) should conduct a formal or informal hearing to consider evidence of a violation and to provide the resident the opportunity to offer a defense against the charge. You must conduct a hearing, or provide an opportunity for the offender to be heard, before you can impose a penalty. However, imposing a penalty shouldn't be your goal—remember, you want to gain compliance. See the sample script for conducting a hearing at the end of this chapter.

Representation. An important part of due process is the right of all parties to be represented by legal counsel. That doesn't mean the association's attorney needs to be present for every hearing to represent the association; however, if you know that a resident is bringing his or her lawyer to a hearing, it probably would be wise for the association to do the same.

Due process merely requires a fair procedure, not necessarily a court-type proceeding. Therefore, keep your hearing simple and informal. Don't confront or cross-examine. Give the resident an opportunity to explain, and don't let yourself be drawn into an argument. Keep an open mind, and make every effort to reach an understanding. A sample script for conducting a hearing can be found at the end of this chapter.

> *People are always making rules for themselves and always finding loopholes.*
>
> —*William Rotsler*

> *Good people do not need laws to tell them to act responsibly, while bad people will find a way around the laws.*
>
> —*Plato*

When violations are based on a resident's complaint, such as excessive noise, you should require the resident who made the complaint to appear at the hearing.

Decision. When you've made the decision, issue the determination. Some state statutes require associations to issue the decision within a specified time. Send the findings—good news or bad—in writing, remembering again that a positive tone is important.

Appeal. Provide an opportunity for the alleged violator to appeal from an adverse decision. In the spirit of a true appeal, a different group of people should hear the appeal and report their findings to the board for reconsideration of the original decision.

How To Conduct a Hearing

DO	DON'T
❏ Keep it simple and informal.	❏ Don't use a court-like setting.
❏ State the case against the resident.	❏ Don't confront or cross-examine the resident.
❏ Let the resident respond in his or her own words.	❏ Don't engage in argument.
❏ Listen carefully to the resident's explanation.	❏ Don't ask questions unless you need clarification.
❏ Require complainants to attend the hearing.	❏ Don't act on anonymous complaints that place the association in the role of accuser.
❏ Obtain compliance.	❏ Don't inflict punishment.

Consequences

What happens when the association and the resident have concluded the hearing and still remain in opposition? What steps should you take to gain compliance? The association can impose monetary consequences—which work very well with some residents—or it may suspend privileges for those who don't respond when hit in the wallet.

Monetary Consequences

The governing documents and the statutes that govern your community may identify possible remedies and sanctions. Some state statutes and governing documents grant authority to the community association to impose monetary charges against an owner for violations of recorded covenants or adopted rules and regulations. Ask your attorney about the laws that apply to your community. For example, the Virginia Condominium Act and the Virginia Property Owners Association Act authorize an association to impose a fine of $50 for a one-time violation or $10 per day for ongoing violations up to 90 days or $1,900. Under such statutes, the money is collectible in the same way that an association collects assessments.

Suspending Privileges

The laws of some jurisdictions as well as some governing documents allow community associations to suspend an owner's right to vote or to use facilities or services, including utilities, offered by the association. Such action is permissible as long as access to the owner's property through the common property is not precluded and the suspension doesn't endanger the health, safety, or property of any resident.

Suspending privileges can be very useful because it has a more immediate effect than imposing monetary consequences. The inconvenience of having a parking pass revoked motivates residents to comply with rules or otherwise resolve the situation. The resident who can ignore a fine will find it much harder to ignore that the cable has been cut off.

Be sure that your association adopts a policy resolution expressly enacting the power to suspend privileges.

Unacceptable Consequences

Since the goal of all compliance efforts is to get residents to understand and abide by the rules, fines and suspensions might be counterproductive. Then, the likely consequences of these and other punitive methods become unacceptable. They're unacceptable simply because they are contrary to the objective of achieving compliance and because they cause more problems than they solve.

For example, an association might choose to publish the names of residents who don't comply with rules. Why? Because some residents will do their best to comply with rules to avoid the embarrassment of being branded a violator. Embarrassing residents may be very effective in gaining compliance, but the cost to the association is unnecessarily high—and includes ill will and potential claims for damages if the information is out of date, no longer true, or not based on fact. Internal due-process proceedings are a better alternative; think about other ways to encourage compliance. As long as they aren't negative, such means for gaining compliance don't create bad feelings among residents or animosity toward the association.

Alternative Dispute Resolution

Occasionally compliance will prove to be untenable, or a problem intractable. Maybe fines have failed to spur compliance, or revoking privileges hasn't gotten the resident's attention, and now you're considering legal action. Before taking that final step, the association should consider seeking professional assistance.

Invite the resident and his or her attorney to participate in some form of alternative dispute resolution (ADR) with the association and its counsel. Internal due process is a form of ADR, but there are other, more generally recognized mechanisms that are equally applicable to community associations. The model ethical rules for the legal profession adopted in many jurisdictions dictate that lawyers must counsel

> *He is a benefactor of mankind who contracts the great rules of life into short sentences that may be easily impressed on the memory, and so recur habitually to the mind.*
>
> *—Samuel Johnson*

> *I made a game effort to argue but two things were against me: the umpires and the rules.*
>
> —Leo Durocher

their clients to consider alternative dispute resolution. So, not only is ADR a good idea, it may be mandated.

Essentially, there are two methods of alternative dispute resolution—mediation and arbitration.

Mediation

In mediation, both parties meet with a mediator or facilitator who helps them reach a mutually agreeable settlement. The settlement, which the parties arrive at themselves, is incorporated into an enforceable, legal contract. Typically, mediators charge per hour for their services, and the parties agree beforehand to split those costs. Mediation is an excellent method for resolving disputes where the relationship is long-term, such as between the association and a resident.

Rather than being the last resort, mediation can also be an effective first step. For example, if a resident asks the association to take action against a neighbor, rather than viewing the situation as a compliance issue, the association might first bring in a mediator to talk to the two parties. By facilitating a solution between the two neighbors, the association has solved the problem reasonably, without having to be the enforcer.

Where to Find a Mediator

- **Check your local phone directory.**
- **Call the clerk of the small-claims court for a reference.**
- **Call the consumer-complaint division of the district attorney's or commonwealth's office.**
- **Call the American Arbitration Association.**

Arbitration

In arbitration, the parties retain the services of a professional arbitrator. Associations should seek arbitrators who are licensed members of the American Arbitration Association or individuals familiar with community associations.

In this non-judicial process, the arbitrator acts as a judge, listening to the testimony and evidence of both parties. Following the presentation of the evidence, the arbitrator decides the case in favor of one of the parties. In most cases, the parties agree beforehand to bind themselves to the arbitrator's decision.

As with mediation, the parties typically split the cost. Some arbitrators charge on an hourly basis, but this should be discussed before the arbitration begins.

Alternative dispute resolution may spare the association significant legal expenses and court costs. However, both parties must be willing to participate in this option and to share the legal fees associated with this process. That can be problematic. Moreover, if the association does not consider compromise a viable option, ADR may not be a practical solution to the association's predicament.

Since the courts favor and encourage ADR, association boards should take the opportunity to resolve the dispute in this manner before pursuing judicial enforcement.

Using the Judicial System to Achieve Compliance

As a last resort, you may have to take legal action against residents to get them to comply with rules. If this is the case, it's best to follow the counsel of your association attorney. Advice on how to be reasonable once a suit is filed is beyond the scope of this book—but that doesn't mean that being reasonable is beyond the scope of the association. Let your attorney know that the association strives to be reasonable in all proceedings, and work together to attain compliance.

Sample Script: Due-Process Hearing

Good evening, and thank you for attending this hearing before the board of the _____
Association on [*Specify the date.*]

I'm_____,
the association president. With me at the table are other members of the association board: [*Name each board member.*]

Also, at the table are: [*Name others and specify their role, such as architectural committee chair, staff members, etc.*]

Association legal counsel, _____,
is also present and will assist us in conducting the hearing.

This hearing is based on authority set forth in a policy resolution adopted by the board pursuant to the _____Act, and more specifically, Section(s) _____ of the Act. Under the policy and these statutory provisions, the board has the authority to assess charges against any association member for any violation of the declaration or rules and regulations for which the member or his or her family members, tenants, guests, or other invitees are responsible.

Before these charges may be assessed, however, the law requires that the resident be given notice and this opportunity for a hearing.

At this time, I ask that each participant identify himself or herself: [*Pause for introductions.*]

I now ask you to confirm that you received notice of this proceeding. [*Pause for responses.*]

Let me explain how the hearing will proceed. We will adhere to the following schedule:

Continued on next page

Continued from previous page

1. Mr./Ms. _____ ,
speaking on behalf of the association, will present the facts in this
case as they have been determined by _____
_____. (5 minutes).

2. Mr./Ms. _____ ,
resident, will address the board regarding the allegations.
(5 minutes).

3. Mr./Ms. _____ ,
speaking on behalf of the association, will present a rebuttal, and
ask questions of the board, and answer questions from the board.
(5 minutes).

4. Mr./Ms. _____ ,
resident, will present a rebuttal, and ask questions of the board,
and answer questions from the board. (5 minutes).

This is a total of 20 minutes to hear testimony. We are imposing the
time limitations to assure that the hearing moves along. However, if
at any time you have questions or concerns, please be sure to raise
them.

**5. The board will recess into executive session to consider the pre-
sentations of all participants.**

**6. The board will reconvene into open session to take a vote on the
matter. Participants are welcome to remain until the board recon-
venes in open session to hear any motions that are made.
Additionally, the** _____
[*specify manager, secretary, other*] **will notify you in writing of the
decision within** _____ **working days of this meeting.**

Our purpose this evening is to ensure that you, the resident, have a
full and fair opportunity to present information concerning the
alleged violations.

• Do you understand these proceedings as I have outlined them?

• Again, for the record, did you receive notice of this proceeding?

• Do you understand the allegations as set forth in the notice?

Then we are ready to begin. [*Begin with item 1.*]

There are those whose sole claim to profundity is the discovery of exceptions to THE RULES.

—*Paul Eldridge*

chapter five

Educating Residents About Rules

T he best rules in the world won't do your association any good if your residents don't know about them. Educating residents is a continuous process, and its importance cannot be underestimated. The more you inform your residents about the rules—what they are, why they're important, what happens when they're not observed— the fewer rules will be broken and the less effort you'll have to expend to achieve compliance.

Delivering the Information

Use as many avenues of delivery as possible to educate residents about the rules—resale packages, association handbooks, orientations, newsletters, Web sites, flyers, and resident handbooks.

Try to reach prospective buyers *before* they go to settlement. Local real-estate agents are your first line of contact. Provide them with information about your association in a letter or a brochure, and make it available on your Web site as well. Your letter or brochure should include your Web address so that prospective buyers can learn more about your community *and* access your full set of rules—before they move in.

Also, provide real-estate agents with the name of a board member or manager whom prospective buyers can contact for more informa-tion, and ask them to mention to their clients the importance of read-ing everything in the resale package. Choose your association contact carefully! This person can be a positive or negative.

You may even consider holding an annual "home fair" or community-wide open house for real-estate agents who specialize in listing and sell-ing homes in your community association. Not only is a home fair a great way to market the community, it's a great way to educate home-owners and their agents about rules—their benefits and their impact on preserving value and promoting community.

> *The ideas I stand for are not mine. I borrowed them from Socrates. I swiped them from Chesterfield. I stole them from Jesus. And I put them in a book. If you don't like their rules, whose would you use?*
>
> —*Dale Carnegie*

Resale Packages and Association Handbooks

All too often, a new buyer's first exposure to the association is the resale package—which, unfortunately, sometimes arrives as late as settlement. If the law of your jurisdiction requires resale disclosure, be sure to get it to the purchaser as soon as possible.

Of course, even if purchasers receive resale information ahead of time, buying a new home and moving are such major life events that they'll probably have little time or inclination to read the fine print in all those documents. Many don't even know they've received them.

What's more, because the law typically mandates the contents of resale packages, the information can be legally focused—that is, boring. It may not be a good idea to include anything that isn't required by law—although association rules are usually among the required contents of the resale package. So, consider developing an association handbook separate from the resale package, to be given to each resident as a welcome to the community. The handbook can contain the same information as the resale package—and much more.

In either case—whether you provide a resale package or a handbook—make the information inviting. But, how do you get new homeowners' attention at a time when they're least likely to give it?

Make it attractive. New residents will take one look at numerous documents stuffed into an 8x12 envelope at settlement and figure they're just more red tape. When they do get around to looking at the package, the envelope will be tossed, and the documents will be separated or lost.

Getting Past the Red Tape

If you send your resale package in an envelope, include a teaser on the outside that will motivate new residents to open it.

- **"Congratulations! You're moving into a National Community Association of the Year Award winner. Details enclosed."**
- **"Pool passes enclosed."**
- **"Will your car be towed tonight? See the enclosed parking policy."**
- **"You're invited to a neighborhood party—invitation enclosed."**
- **"If you read only one thing in this envelope, make it The Rules."**

Avoid the red-tape connotation by putting all documents in a binder with your association logo, name, address, and phone number on it. Check the local yellow pages for a printer who specializes in imprinted binders, or buy some binders at an office-supply store, and slip a cover page into the front of each one. People do judge books by their covers, so an attractive binder or similar presentation will be taken more seriously than an envelope full of stapled copies of fine print.

Make it reader friendly. Whether it's in an envelope or a binder, make sure the content of your package follows a few simple rules as well:

Documents should look professional and uniform. Each document should follow the same format or style of presentation. Also, make sure each one is readable and professional in presentation. Avoid using copies of copies.

The Reader-Friendly Test for Resale Packages

❏ Are all documents uniform? Same type face, same size font, same margins?

❏ Do all pages *look like* originals?

❏ Are all pages clear and easy to read?

❏ Does every page contain the association name, phone number, and address?

❏ Does the package have a table of contents, a subject matter index, and section tabs?

Provide a table of contents—that kind of organization helps the reader focus on what's important. (Believe it or not, the rules are important to new members of community associations.) Use index tabs to make it easy for the reader to find the information listed on the contents page. A topical index is a good companion, too—then the resale package or association handbook will become a reference work for the new homeowner or resident.

Make it independent. Each document should be able to stand alone. If you choose to use an envelope, minimize the problems that will occur when the documents are eventually scattered by including the association name and contact information on each one. This is also true if you use a binder, since sections of the binder may be removed. If each document can't stand alone—your handbook is a bound volume, for example—cross-reference the documents, and make sure they're accurate and clear.

Make it easy. If your rules are scattered throughout the documents in the resale package—some in resolutions, some in the bylaws, some in policies—pull them out into one simple list of rules, and place that list first in the package. Call it a "Summary of Rules" and reference the document where the complete version can be found.

New Resident Orientations

A good way to welcome new members of the community is to conduct periodic or personal orientations. These can be formal group reception or one-on-one social calls. Spend a few moments saying hello to new residents, and in the process give them helpful information about living in the community. This will enrich their enjoyment of their new home. It will also give you time to talk about rules and the expectations of fellow residents.

Sometimes being anonymous makes it easier to disregard rules. When you go out of your way to meet new residents, they lose their

> *The young man knows the rules, but the old man knows the exceptions.*
>
> —Oliver Wendell Holmes

> *The only thing I believe is this: A player does not have to like a manager and he does not have to respect a manager. All he has to do is obey the rules.*
>
> —Sparky Anderson

anonymity and will be less likely to ignore a rule. Also, you cannot expect residents to comply with a rule they know nothing about; make sure they know something about the rule through a new resident orientation.

Sample Agenda for New Resident Orientation

I.   Introduction of association staff and volunteer leaders
II. Review services provided by association
     Trash removal, common-area maintenance, in-unit services program, social programs
III. Property tour
IV. Association governance structure
     Board, committees
V.   Board meeting schedule
VI. Financial information
     Association budget, assessment requirements
VII. Association rules
     Move-in, pets, parking

Constant Reminders

Even new owners who have actually read the rules will likely file the resale package away with their other settlement documents. So it's likely that distributing your rules once won't ensure compliance. Even those who attended the new resident orientation will need a reminder from time to time.

Education is a process, and repetition is its foundation. Here are some ways to educate residents about the rules continuously.

Newsletters

According to a study conducted by the Gallup Organization, 93 percent of the people who receive a community association newsletter read it all or most of the time. That makes your newsletter a great place to remind residents of rules—all of them, or just one or two that are ignored regularly.

Create a "Rule Reminder" column in your newsletter. Highlight a different rule in each issue, or ask for feedback about rules that are under consideration. Use the column to explain a rule—noting, for example, that the association isn't just being contrary by disallowing open-flame grills on balconies, the county fire ordinance prohibits it.

Signs

In some circumstances, the association can post rules creatively and permanently using signs. For example, "Parking By Permit Only" can be stenciled on blacktop and "No Dumping" on the recycling bins.

Post your pool rules on the side of the pool house. Use sandwich boards or portable marquees to post temporary reminders in problem areas: "Remember to pick up after your pet."

Handbooks

No association handbook is complete without a section on rules. Spell them out in easy-to-understand language. Most will come from or be supported by your governing documents and local and state law. Include the exact wording, and add a paraphrase if necessary to clarify a point. Cite the authority for each rule so residents understand the association or board hasn't imposed anything arbitrarily. You may want to go a step further and include a rationale for some or all of the rules, particularly those that seem unusual.

Some of the rules may exist in the form of resolutions or policies, such as for parking or assessments. Include these as well. If the language is too formal, summarize the specific points of compliance in a bulleted list.

Web sites

All information about your rules—the resale package, resident handbook, newsletter articles, or policies—can and should be placed on your Web site. Make these things easy to find.

Others

These are only a few ways to remind residents of association rules. There are dozens more. Remember, unique and creative rule reminders—like clever commercials—effectively leave a message in a resident's mind. For example, one Virginia community welcomed new residents to the community with a gift—a pooper scooper containing the message "Please clean up after your pet. It's our rule."

Special Considerations

It's in your association's best interest to see that every resident understands the rules. Take into consideration the special needs of all your residents when you publish information about rules. For example, how many and which languages are commonly used among residents in your association—including American Sign? If the percentage is significant, consider making information available in more than one language.

You may be able to enlist your residents to supervise or provide the translation and distribution. If you go this route, have a professional translator review the documents for accuracy before putting the association's name on them. It would be useful if the English-language documents that are recorded contain notice that unrecorded versions are available in other languages from the association.

The question of who pays for these services will come up. There's no right answer. It will depend on how many people need the services, how much the association will benefit from the improved communication,

You are remembered for the rules you break.

—Gen. Douglas MacArthur

41

> *The young break rules for fun. The old for profit.*
>
> —*Mason Cooley*

what resources the community has, and numerous other factors. Fees for a professional to review a translation, or actually do the translating, might qualify as common expenses; check with your attorney or accountant to determine the best way to cover them.

In some communities, residents might appreciate large-print editions of the rules and governing documents. Word processing software makes it very easy to reformat documents using large print. For other associations, an American Sign translator might be an invaluable addition at annual meetings, board meetings, or hearings.

Sometimes an audio presentation can be helpful—for those who may comprehend the spoken word better than the printed word, for those with weak reading skills, and for those who are simply very busy. Consider making an audio tape of the association rules—with commentary on why the rules are important, how they were developed, what residents like about them—for busy commuters to listen to in the car or for those who just need an alternative to the printed page.

* * * * *

Ignorance of the rules is probably the main reason residents break them. It's the association's job to be proactive in educating residents—all residents, not just owners—about the standards of the community. This one accomplishment will contribute more to voluntary compliance with rules than any other action the association can undertake.

INTEGRITY
has no need of rules.

—Albert Camus

chapter six

Accommodating the Pink Flamingo

Whence all your committees have been convened, your residents notified, your resolutions signed, and your rules canonized, you settle into the day-to-day operating and governing of the community. On a practical level, what can and should you do to be truly reasonable, to get along, and to promote harmony, community, and just plain neighborly good will? In this chapter, we'll look at practical strategies for developing specific rules.

All examples in this chapter are real, unfortunately. They have been culled from existing CC&Rs of numerous community associations.

Strategies for Being Reasonable About Children
- Focus on behavior, not age.
- Be positive and communicate with parents or guardians.
- Involve residents of all ages in the community.

Common sense—not to mention common law—says that parents are responsible for the actions of their children. If your association subscribes to the basic principles that rules should apply to *all* residents and that rules should regulate *behavior*, then singling out particular groups—like children—isn't necessary, and may even be illegal.

An Example
Parents will direct and control the activities of their children in order to require them to conform to the regulations. Parents will be responsible for violations or damage caused by their children whether or not the parents are present.

This rule is legal, even reasonable, but it's neither friendly nor positive. Words like "direct," "control," "require," and "conform" don't promote harmony. They're intended to show that you mean business, but that can more appropriately be demonstrated through even-handed, consistent

> *Civilization had too many rules for me, so I did my best to rewrite them.*
>
> —*Bill Cosby*

enforcement. And, by singling out children, it ignores the behavior of adult family members who may be in someone else's care—such as Alzheimer's sufferers.

An Alternative
Residents of *all ages* must abide by the association's rules for the safety and enjoyment of all. Parents and guardians should familiarize all members of the household with these rules and ensure that they abide by them.

Focus on Behavior, Not Age
Your rules should specify appropriate behavior or prohibited behavior. Don't assume that only children are loud or destructive or incompetent. For example, "Children under 8 are not allowed in the pool" is discriminatory, but "Swimmers must demonstrate proficiency or swim with a companion," is entirely appropriate.

Be Positive and Communicate With Parents or Guardians
Inevitably a kid will break a window or ride a bike across the lawn. Often just alerting the parent to a situation is sufficient. Whenever possible, work with parents or guardians to correct the problem.

Involve Residents of All Ages in the Community
Implement age-appropriate activities that make all residents—youngsters and seniors—feel like real community members. For example, if your association has a relatively high number of adolescents, consider creating a youth committee or appoint a youth adviser to the board. Other types of advisers can be appointed to the board in an effort to gain the perspective of particular demographic groups—such as retired residents, non-resident owners, or seasonal residents.

Facilitate Compliance
- Provide an opportunity for errant residents to perform community service to pay a repair bill or fine.
- "Fine" school-age offenders by having them write an article about sidewalk safety or the origin of graffiti for the community newsletter.
- Ask the offender to organize a clean-up effort, or to work with an association committee to landscape the very flower bed that has been trampled.

If the issue is safety and stems from *where* residents (usually children, but not always) play—in the street, for example—consider a few accommodations before enacting a ban or prohibition.
- Lower the speed limit or install traffic-calming measures like speed bumps in appropriate areas.
- Install signs with "Caution: Children Playing" and other warnings on the community's streets.

- If possible, designate a playing field, construct a playground, or find other outlets for high-energy activity.

Strategies for Being Reasonable About Pets
- Avoid restrictions based on size and weight.
- Comply with local ordinances.
- Form a pet committee.
- Take advantage of other resources.
- Be flexible.

Pets don't have to be a problem for your community association—as long as your pet rules are reasonable and allow for some flexibility, and as long as you remember that pet rules are about people with pets, not just pets.

An Example
No animals, birds, or reptiles of any kind will be raised, bred, or kept, except for: no more than one dog less than 20 inches in height at the shoulder at maturity and of gentle disposition; no more than two cats, usual domestic birds in cages and fish in tanks, or other household pets approved by the executive board or the manager as to compatibility with the community.

This rule is not unusual for communities wishing to restrict the number of pets. However, it presents some enforcement challenges. The first, of course, is the 20-inch limit; and the second is that terms like "gentle disposition" and "compatibility with the community" are subject to a wide range of interpretations. Additionally, it's pointless to specify the number of pets allowed inside a unit since it's unlikely that noncompliance will be noticed.

An Alternative
No animals, birds, or reptiles of any kind will be raised, bred, or kept, except for usual household pets including dogs, cats, domestic birds in cages, and fish in tanks.

Avoid Restrictions Based on Size and Weight
Many associations restrict pets according to size—either by weight or height—or by breed. However, these types of restrictions ignore a more fundamental issue: the behavior of the pet (usually a dog) and its owner. Instead, your rules should address the undesirable behavior of any animal (attacking, biting, jumping), regardless of size, weight, or breed.

Also, size restrictions are difficult to monitor and very difficult to enforce. Who is going to weigh or measure the pets? When? How often? Would it be reasonable to evict a pet because it was one pound or one inch over the limit? If you didn't enforce the size restrictions, you might as well not have them. In fact, that's a good idea. Don't have them.

> *It is all very well to have principles, rules of behavior concerning right and wrong. But it is quite as essential to know when to forget, as when to use them.*
>
> —Alice Foote MacDougall

Comply With Local Ordinances

Association pet rules should support and proceed from your basic local animal ordinance—usually to leash, license, and scoop. Requiring up-to-date immunizations is also reasonable.

Form a Pets Committee

Delegate pet-related matters to a pets committee. Committee members should represent both pet owners and non-owners, and they should be moderate and reasonable—not strongly biased for or against pets. Even if your pet rules are in good shape, a pets committee can consider requests for waivers, sit in on violation hearings and waiver hearings, issue citations for rule violations, and address complaints. Pets committee members can also write articles for your newsletter that highlight association rules and suggest ways to comply with them.

Take Advantage of Other Resources

In some areas, the Humane Society or the SPCA provides animal-control services under contract to local governments. But even if they don't, they always offer resources to help with pet problems and should be considered as a possible ally in achieving compliance with your rules.

Large pet stores also offer numerous resources, and may be helpful. For example, they may conduct training workshops in your community, provide discount inoculations, make presentations at an annual meeting, or work with your pets committee to solve specific problems.

Be Flexible

One way to be reasonable with pet rules is to recognize that pets can't be controlled as easily as the color of the shutters or the spot where the car is parked. Of course, this doesn't mean that animals should be allowed to run wild, either. Just recognize that your residents' emotional bonds with their pets are real and very strong. Ruling that a troublesome pet must go isn't at all reasonable as far as the owner is concerned. Nor is it always necessary; the association can take positive steps to facilitate compliance with pet rules and promote good will within the community at the same time:

Facilitate Compliance

- Require insurance and warranties. One of the reasons that associations restrict pets by size is the belief that the bigger the dog, the more damage it can do. If damage is the issue, and you'd prefer to stick with size limits, allow residents to keep pets that exceed the limit if those pets are covered by a pet warranty. Pet warranties are similar to insurance but cover only property damage, not liability. A number of real-estate service providers offer them to supplement pet deposits. Your pet policy should spell out the behavior that will trigger the requirement for a warranty.

    Another option is requiring the pet owner to obtain pet-liability insurance, which can protect the association, augment enforcement procedures, and allow residents to keep their pets. This insurance should not be confused with homeowners insurance, which may not cover pet damage or liability. These policies are relatively inexpensive and are available online from such providers as *RentWithPets.com*, sponsored by the Humane Society of the United States, and *LeaseWithPets.com*.

- Require obedience training. Pet rules should take into account the behavior of both animals and their owners. Your enforcement methods should be sensitive to that mindset as well, and try to help owners and pets alike. For example, before you evict an obnoxious pet, require the owner to attend obedience training with the pet and provide the association proof of completion. If the objectionable behavior continues, even after proper training, consider other enforcement methods.

- Ask the local animal shelter to participate in an association-sponsored vaccination and licensing event. When residents show up for their reduced-fee rabies inoculation, ask them to complete the association's pet-registration form, hand them a copy of the pet rules, and distribute plastic pick-up bags.

- A registration program is a great way to know the pets in your community—and it may be important in emergency situations to know where the pets are. Registration programs also serve as a way to obtain the assurances you need that all your pets are properly inoculated and licensed, or that their owners have obtained the proper warranty or insurance.

- Inconvenience seems to be the biggest reason people don't pick up after their dogs. So, make it convenient. Place containers of disposable pooper scoopers throughout the community. Dog walkers won't have to carry their own scoopers or bags, and they can dispose of waste in handy bins next to the bag dispensers.

- Compile a list of dog walkers and pet sitters in your community, and make it available to residents.

- If possible, provide a designated outdoor area where pets can exercise or play. Ask dog owners to maintain it or pay a nominal fee for its use and upkeep.

- Look outside your community for help. Many cities have free programs or provide mediators specifically for pet problems. The San Francisco SPCA, for example, offers this service through its "Open Door" program.

Strategies for Being Reasonable About Flags
- Suspend flag restrictions temporarily.
- Distinguish between U.S. flags, others flags, and poles.
- Tailor rules accordingly.

Flags have long been a source of controversy for community associations. The popularity of decorative, seasonal flags is usually the original source of any limitations. While those seasonal banners have been

> *Learn to play the game of life…according to the rules of society. If you can put that into practice in the community in which you live, then, to me you have won the greatest championship.*
>
> —Jesse Owens

> *The rules were such that it was actually not possible for me to keep them.*
>
> —*George Orwell*

eclipsed by more vigorous patriotic expression, some governing documents still prohibit flags altogether or restrict their size, placement, or height in an effort to maintain uniformity in the community, avoid property damage, or maintain safety.

Sometimes the real issue is excessive size or the height of the pole, but the focus of the media and often the general public usually ends up on the flag itself and the question of individual expression. This is because these days the flags in question are almost always U.S. flags. Inevitably, the issue swings from protecting property toward patriotism and pride.

Recent events have challenged community associations to approach the flag issue less dogmatically. Patriotism is ascending throughout the country and prohibiting or restricting its demonstration is unpopular—and often unreasonable.

An Example
Flag poles, whether free-standing or surface mounted are prohibited.

This is one of those rules that produces unintentional results. Residents in this community who wish to fly a flag may simply suspend it from a railing or eave, display it in a window, or erect a makeshift apparatus that doesn't quite qualify as a "pole"—in each case likely bumping up against another prohibition such as draping items over the balcony.

An Alternative
Free standing, base-mounted flag poles are prohibited; however, flagpoles up to 6 feet in length may be mounted externally to a unit in accordance with the safety and architectural standards specified in Section II for the purposes of flying the U.S. flag and state flags.

Suspend Flag Restrictions Temporarily
In light of the fact that the U.S. Congress passed a resolution in September 2001 encouraging Americans to fly the American flag, outright bans may be outdated.

If your association prohibits the flying of flags, talk to your community members about the policy. Suspend enforcement of any restrictions during the debate. Convene a committee to review your flag rules, particularly in light of the heightened sense of patriotism among Americans brought on by recent events. Charge the committee with finding acceptable ways for residents to demonstrate their patriotism—especially flying flags—in ways that don't damage property, impose on neighbors, or offend the patriotism of others. There are strict rules of etiquette for flying the flag that some flag wavers overlook. Why not incorporate those rules into your own?

This doesn't mean that rules on how and where to fly American flags should be tossed out. Or that rules intended to eliminate property damage should be ignored. Ask the committee to draft amendments or suggest new rules that achieve these goals.

Distinguish Between U.S. Flags, Others Flags, and Poles

Review and redraft, if necessary, flag rules so that it's clear that your residents' rights to express their patriotism are supported by the association, that the association supports the congressional resolution to fly the American flag, and that different restrictions may apply to flags other than the U.S. flag. Your rule should also specify acceptable height, placement, and methods of erecting poles—if poles are allowed at all.

Tailor Rules Accordingly

Flag rules that are appropriate for homeowner associations may not work for a condominium association. Noise, aesthetics, uniform appearance, and safety are all factors that vary depending on whether a flagpole is erected in the yard of a single-family home or the common areas of a condominium.

Facilitate Compliance

- Let residents know that the association's goal is to balance the rights of residents to express themselves with the obligation of the association to protect property by prescribing how and when flags may be displayed, where poles may be erected or attached, and what types of flags are acceptable.
- Provide information to all residents on the manner in which U.S. flags should be displayed. You can find it on the Web by entering "Federal Flag Code" in your Web browser.
- Provide alternative ways for residents to demonstrate patriotism. The same committee that reviews and possibly rewrites the flag rules might also be the appropriate group to recommend association-sponsored activities for all residents. Fourth of July or Memorial Day picnics, Flag Day contests, blood drives, relief-effort fund-raising events, or Veteran's Day observances are just a few ideas.
- Compromise. If your association has a ban on flying flags, consider allowing limited exceptions on appropriate days—Memorial Day, Flag Day, the Fourth of July, and Veteran's Day.

Strategies for Being Reasonable About Design Review

- Make it a benefit, not a burden.
- Establish reasonable guidelines.
- Establish a design review committee.
- Process applications promptly.

Design review or architectural controls are a benefit to the entire community because they protect property values and keep the community looking attractive. These controls exists as much to protect a neighbor

> *Laws, to be just, must give a reciprocation of rights; without this, they are mere arbitrary rules of conduct, founded in force, and not in conscience.*
>
> —*Thomas Jefferson*

> *The United States Constitution has proved itself the most marvelously elastic compilation of rules of government ever written.*
>
> *—Franklin D. Roosevelt*

from the home-improvement fanatic next door as to say no to the well-intentioned builder.

An Example

1. Homeowners may repaint their house to the existing paint color, as long as the existing paint color is on the approved paint color charts provided and approved by the association. If the existing paint color is not an approved color, the procedure outlined in #2 below must be followed.

2. Paint color changes must be on the paint color charts provided by the association and must be processed and approved by the review process procedure outlined in Section III.

Section III. All applications for alterations shall include the following information: site plan/plat of your property and adjacent properties; architectural drawing and/or picture of proposed alteration, including dimensions; color, including paint chip of proposed paint; description of materials; estimated start and completion dates.

This rules almost dares a resident to comply with the approved color scheme. Consider: If the existing paint color *isn't* on the approved list, it's not in compliance. Presumably, the resident wishes to repaint in order to correct the problem. However, according to this set of guidelines, the resident has to go through the entire application process in order to paint his or her home an *approved* color.

An Alternative

1. Homeowners may paint the exteriors of their homes only with those colors listed on the association's approved paint color charts. Paint color changes are subject to the review process outlined in Section III.

Section III. Applications for alterations (except repainting) shall include … Applications for repainting shall include the address of the property being repainted; a description or diagram of areas to be painted; color, including paint chip; colors of adjacent properties; and estimated start and completion dates.

Make It a Benefit, Not a Burden

Design review procedures and requirements should be moderate, not unduly restrictive, and reasonable. The process should be a positive, cooperative endeavor between resident and association.

Establish Reasonable Guidelines

Architectural guidelines are themselves rules—so, apply the processes outlined in other chapters for adopting or amending them. Include a workable system for the design review process that clarifies or expands on the governing documents, and thereby lets residents know what's expected. Make sure that your guidelines are up-to-date. For example, if your guidelines establish an exterior color palette, make sure that the paint color is still available.

Establish a Design Review Committee

Depending on the size of your community and the number of applications you receive, a design review committee may be a necessity. Select residents who represent a variety of interests and contribute differing expertise. Also, make sure your volunteers are fair-minded, willing to compromise, and able to work through a challenging situation. Not everyone on the committee needs to be an architect, engineer, or builder, nor should they be. However, at least one person with expertise in this area could be an asset.

Provide the committee with criteria for decision making (including the flexibility to grant variances), procedures for processing applications, and standards to follow. Keep good records of decisions made— so you have clear precedent on which to rely.

Process Applications Promptly

One Virginia association has architectural guidelines that specify, "Failure of the board to approve or disapprove a request within 60 days shall be construed as board approval of the request." Does that mean the board has two months to make a decision? No. Home improvements can be time-sensitive; some activities are best undertaken at certain times of the year, and the do-it-yourselfer may be planning a big project during an already-scheduled vacation. Therefore, it's important to process applications promptly in order to maintain goodwill and to prevent residents from sidestepping the review process.

Make sure the application is complete and that the applicant and reviewer understand the proposed improvement. Many dicey architectural cases arise out of a misunderstanding about what was approved. Use diagrams and ask questions, so that everyone has a clear understanding of the proposal.

Facilitate Compliance

- Conduct a workshop. The first step in attaining compliance is educating residents about the value of architectural control—the why. The "how" is just as important, and may benefit from a more direct approach. Consider providing information that helps residents design the proposed improvement according to the guidelines, and that makes the application process simple. An annual workshop on the process, led by a successful applicant, could be a real help to prospective applicants.
- Add to your architectural guidelines examples of the types of changes or improvements that need approval, the procedures for

Each problem that I solved became a rule which served afterwards to solve other problems.

—Rene Descartes

53

> *There is all the difference in the world between departure from recognized rules by one who has learned to obey them, and neglect of them through want of training or want of skill or want of understanding.*
>
> —*Ellen Terry*

applying (include application forms, if you require them), the criteria for approval that will be used to decide the request, and other design considerations.

- Keep problem solving and positive results in mind—not penalties.
- Be moderate. Inflexibility on the part of the association may pit neighbor against neighbor.
- Accept all requests, even from residents who are already in violation.
- Don't refuse to consider a request because of an existing unapproved change.
- Don't automatically require residents to take down unauthorized structures as a condition of review.

Strategies for Being Reasonable About Parking
- Consider residents' lifestyles.
- Be flexible.
- Avoid towing except in emergencies.
- Mind your fair housing P's and Q's.

Parking is one of those hot-button issues that continually challenge associations. Few developers ever opt for more than the minimum required number of parking spaces when building a community. But, it's the association that has to grapple with the overcrowding. There are other parking issues, too, but take heart. It's possible to find a workable parking plan. Design the one that makes sense for your community.

An Example
No truck, bus, or commercial vehicle of any kind shall be permitted to be kept or parked overnight on the property or on the adjoining streets.

This rule is problematic for several reasons. First, it is unduly restrictive. Conventional passenger cars no longer comprise the majority of vehicles in use today. Second, the terms "truck, bus, or commercial vehicle" will undoubtedly lead to wrangling about specific vehicle types. Is a sport utility vehicle a truck? Is a minivan a bus? Is a taxi a commercial vehicle if it's the resident's only transportation? Third, it doesn't look like enforcement is very practical: who patrols the streets at night? How do you know who actually owns the truck on the "adjoining street?" Fourth, this rule is all this townhouse association's documents say about parking; there's no alternative for parking these types of vehicles. And, fifth, this rule leaves many questions unanswered, such as the number and condition of vehicles that can be parked.

An Alternative
Residents may park their primary vehicles on the property and the adjoining streets. Oversized service vehicles and recreational vehicles

should be parked in designated areas. Vehicles must comply with all county and state licensing and registration requirements.

Consider Residents' Lifestyles
Depending on where your association is located, resident lifestyles may have a lot to do with what's reasonable. Rules that disallow parking campers or trucks in the driveway may be appropriate in Chicago, but may be considered unreasonable in Wyoming or Texas.

Be Flexible
If there's a demand for parking campers, service vehicles, or trucks in the community, designate a specific parking area for them. This may be a challenge in communities where developers have specified the number and placement of spaces or haven't provided sufficient undesignated spaces. If the demand is high enough, and the governing documents allow it, consider broadening your definitions of various vehicle types or purposes to allow some flexibility.

For example, for some residents, a service vehicle may double as primary transportation. If the only vehicle Mr. Smith, the self-employed electrician, drives or parks in the community is his service van, making an exception to the no-service-vehicles rule may be more reasonable than requiring Mr. Smith to buy another vehicle that complies with the rule.

Avoid Towing Except in Emergencies
Emergency towing from fire lanes is a must. Towing otherwise should be carefully considered, according to a well-defined procedure and after you've provided notice. Check out your local ordinances, which should have something to say about towing. Be careful about who is authorized to tow. Post signs and warning reminders.

Mind Your Fair Housing P's and Q's
The federal Fair Housing Amendments Act of 1988 requires associations to make "reasonable accommodations" in the rules of the association where necessary to permit a disabled person to use and enjoy their unit and the common areas.

Facilitate Compliance
- Increase the number of parking spaces. Since overcrowding is a big contributor to parking woes, consider re-striping your parking lot to increase the number of spaces. This sometimes can be done by angling the spaces, or adding parallel spaces along roadways. Or, you may even find some medians or extra green space that can be converted.
- Not all vehicles need the same amount of space. Allocate "compact only," "oversized vehicles," or "motorcycle only" spaces.

> *If men make war in slavish obedience to rules, they will fail.*
>
> —*Ulysses S. Grant*

* * * * *

In this chapter we've looked at strategies for being reasonable about a few of the more challenging rules that community associations deal with from day to day. Arguably, there are others—including satellite dishes, holiday decorations, and noise—to name a few. But, these should give you the basic idea. Undoubtedly, you've noticed the general principles of reasonableness running through the advice on each one. Armed with the information in this book and these examples—you can successfully reinvent your own rules creatively and reasonably, and in the process put your community first.

About the Author

Lucia Anna Trigiani, is a partner in the law firm of Troutman Sanders, L.L.P., resident in the Tysons Corner, Virginia, office of the firm. Her practice focus is in the representation of common-interest community associations, but she also has extensive experience in representing developers of common-interest condominium communities, large mixed-use planned communities, and time-share regimes. Prior to entering private practice in 1987, Ms. Trigiani was the property registration administrator for the Virginia Real Estate Board.

Ms. Trigiani recently concluded a term as president of the Washington Metropolitan Chapter of Community Associations Institute. She was a member of the chapter board of directors from 1994 to 2000 and served as treasurer, vice president, and president-elect. She has served on various committees of Community Associations Institute and is currently co-vice chair of the Government and Public Affairs Committee. At CAI's national conference in May 2001, she was recognized for her work in the industry with the Rising Star Award. She has also been the recipient of the Washington Metropolitan Chapter Distinguished Service Award and is a member of the chapter's Hall of Fame. She is a charter fellow of CAI's College of Community Association Lawyers.

Ms. Trigiani has worked with the Virginia Housing Study Commission on several subcommittees tasked with considering issues and legislation affecting community associations. She chairs the Real Estate Council of the Virginia Bar Association and is also a member of the Administrative Law Council. She was appointed by the governor of Virginia as the first citizen member of the Virginia Real Estate Board. She served on the board from 1992 to 1996, including a term as vice chair from 1995 to 1996.

Ms. Trigiani is a 1983 graduate of T.C. Williams School of Law at the University of Richmond. She received her B.A. in 1980 from Saint Mary's College, Notre Dame.

ABOUT CAI

America's leading advocate for responsible communities
Community Associations Institute (CAI) is the only national organization dedicated to fostering vibrant, responsive, competent community associations. Our mission is to assist community associations in promoting harmony, community, and responsible leadership. We believe that by giving board members, managers, and homeowners the knowledge to better run their associations, they can turn "owners" into "neighbors," increasing harmony, and leading to more prosperous, safer communities.

Putting the unity into community
CAI was founded in 1973 as a multi-disciplinary non-profit alliance serving all stakeholders in community associations. We provide education and resources to America's residential condominium, cooperative, and homeowner associations, and to the professionals and suppliers who serve them.

CAI members include all types of association-governed communities, including condominium and homeowner associations, cooperatives, and planned communities of all sizes; individual homeowners; community managers and management firms; builders and developers; accountants, attorneys, lenders, insurance providers, reserve specialists, and other providers of professional services; public officials; and product and service suppliers—all working together to create more livable communities.

CAI has members in chapters throughout the United States and in several foreign countries, but our reach is much greater. Every homeowner in our member associations, and every employee in our member firms, enjoys many of the benefits of CAI membership as well.

The CAI Promise
In CAI, you'll find a friendly and accessible forum to develop relationships, increase your knowledge, and help shape the future of our communities. CAI offers a host of resources that will help you excel.

To find out more about CAI, visit www.caionline.org or call CAI Direct at 888-224-4321 (M–F, 9–6:30 ET).